# LIVERPOOL
## IT ALL CAME TUMBLIN

Published by Brunswick Printing & Publishing Co. Ltd.
Gibraltar Row, King Edward Industrial Estate, Liverpool L3 7HJ
Telephone: 0151-236-4626

Design & Typesetting by Coleman Print Services Ltd, Liverpool.
Printed by Printfine Ltd, Liverpool.

3rd Edition
Revised July 2000

Page 1 & Inside Back Cover: St. Chrysostom Street, Everton 1967.

Back Cover: Demolition of Victoria Square, off Scotland Road 1966.

*F. R. Davies*
*0151 264 0705.*

I would like to express
my sincere thanks to the following:
Janet Smith (Liverpool Archive Dept.), Peter Carradine, Jim Sheldrick,
Ray O'Connor, everyone at Brunswick Publishing and
finally my brother Frank without whose help and encouragement the production of
this book would not have been possible.

This book is dedicated to my wife
Jean and children, Paul, Stephen and Helen.
Also for my mother and the
'Scottie Road' she knew and loved.

## Forewords by Billy Butler and Johnny Kennedy

Greetings—a couple of years ago, Frank O'Connor (whom I'd known since our Cavern days in the 60's) told me he was writing a book about Liverpool, together with his younger brother, Freddy.

I'm delighted to say that these photographs of the old streets, especially my old neighbourhood around Whitefield Road and the obvious research make this book tremendous reading for me.

It's all credit to the lads that this book should stand as a testimony to our very own 'scouse heritage'.

*Bill, Butler*

*It all came tumbling down*—is an absolute must for any 'Scouser'—young or old, near or far.

I'm personally 'made up' to write these few words, as I've known the authors and their family for many years.

The photographs of the old streets, now sadly gone, brought back to me many memories of where I grew up, and of the people who actually did possess 'hearts of gold'. In my opinion this book has captured the spirit of the real Liverpool.

Finally, my gratitude to Frank and Freddy, for not only reminding me of places long forgotten, but for giving us all a permanent record of a by-gone era in the greatest city in the world—our Liverpool.

*Johnny Kennedy*

---

Liverpool has gone through many changes but in the last 20 years those changes have perhaps been more widespread and dramatic than ever before. Much attention has been paid by artists and photographers to the grand city centre buildings which reflect Liverpool's past as the greatest port in the world. This book is about the humbler, vastly more numerous but equally important buildings that were the dwellings and places of recreation of ordinary people. This is an attempt to record what has happened to the places where real scousers lived—the working class people whose labour went to produce the wealth that made nineteenth century Liverpool one of the richest cities in the world.

I have been at times aware of the awkward mixture of pathos and near comedy that has been involved in my attempt to record, over

## Author's Foreword

the last 20 years or so, that ordinary Liverpool as it disappeared before my very eyes. In so many cases it was all I could do to get there with my camera before the bulldozer destroyed the evidence.

# Contents

The development of any city's housing in terms of its styles and locations is inextricably wrapped up with its growth economically. Liverpool might well be described as a late developer. Although it was as early as 1207 that a charter was issued by King John granting Liverpool the status of a borough, it was not until the seventeenth century that Liverpool's expansion began. Nonetheless part of the street system in the city centre dates back to the early thirteenth century. Chapel Street is one of the earliest streets named after a chapel, St Mary Del Quay, which is thought to have been built in the thirteenth century. Nothing remains of the chapel but a similar site is now occupied by the parish church of Our Lady and St Nicholas known for centuries as the 'sailors church', for the Mersey originally flowed right past it at the bottom of Chapel Street.

Other original streets are Dale Street, Tithebarn Street, High Street, Castle Street, Water Street and Old Hall Street and it was this area that first expanded as the importance of Liverpool as a port grew. The first dock, the Old Dock was built at Canning Place in 1715 and subsequent dock building during the eighteenth century included Canning Dock, Salthouse Dock and Georges Dock. The latter, opened in 1771 and enlarged in 1825, covered the area at the Pier Head between James Street and Chapel Street and so these old streets were right at the heart of the new dock system. During the course of the 18th century the number of ships using the port rose from 102 to 4746, a dramatic rise by any standards. In the early and mid eighteenth century Water Street was the fashionable home for the wealthiest of Liverpool's merchants but by the end of the eighteenth century these narrow streets were packed with traders, working from their shops and houses, and a growing number of warehouses. The wealthy began their flight from the centre, first to the Duke Street, Rodney Street and Canning Street area and then onto Upper Parliament Street. They also moved out into some of the outlying villages such as Kirkdale, Everton and Wavertree.

# Liverpool's Development

In the city centre land values soared and the area became the purely commercial centre it is today. Magnificent buildings were erected by businessmen to reflect their success and prestige. This culminated in the construction of the Pier Head group of offices. These were built between 1907 and the First World War on land reclaimed by the filling of Georges Dock. Incidentally the accurate name for this area is still Georges Pier Head named after the dock and a stone pier which projected into the Mersey at this point. There is still a small part called George's Dock Gate where Chapel Street meets the Dock Road. The riverside of the Dock Road is called Goree as it runs past the Pier Head. This strange name derives from a bare rock off Cape Verde island where slaves were gathered awaiting shipment to the plantations of the West Indies. The massive arcaded Goree Warehouses were built here in 1793 only to be destroyed by a fire, said to have lasted 3 months, in 1802. The warehouses were rebuilt but then destroyed during the blitz in 1941. Many fortunes were made in Liverpool through the slave trade and this appalling trade provided the foundations for many shipping lines. Few slaves would ever have reached the port though the Liverpool Advertiser of 1766 carried a notice for a sale of 11 negro slaves to be held at The Exchange Coffee House in Water Street.

Liverpool City Centre, circa 1500. Showing the Original Street Names.

It should not be thought that all was sweetness and light in the centre of early Liverpool. At the beginning of the seventeenth century Liverpool's population is estimated to have been roughly 2000. By 1700 it was only 6000 but by 1801 it had grown to 80,000. Incredibly, in 1831 the figure had soared to 205,000. This population explosion was further boosted in the early and mid nineteenth century by the huge influx of immigrants fleeing from famine conditions in Ireland. Inevitably all of this meant many people lived in appalling conditions of squalor and disease.

Cellars provided homes for many. An investigation in 1790 revealed that in the city centre 2000 cellars were occupied by nearly 7000 people who lived in dark damp rooms with little or no sanitary provisions. The streets off Castle Street and Old Hall Street, at what was then the Northern end of the city, and around Park Lane in the South were infested with these atrocious cellars. It was no doubt the close proximity of the wealthy to such poverty that persuaded the rich to begin their exodus out of the city centre.

During this period and the early 1800s the other main form of slum dwelling, the

# Living in Liverpool

courts, became well established. A court was the central yard, generally about 25 feet long and 10 feet wide, around which was constructed 2, 3 or 4 storey blocks of rooms on all sides. An average sized court generally housed 20 to 30 families. The front might well appear as a fairly ordinary terrace but once one entered the door or alley into the central court the poor conditions became only too obvious. The small windows received little light as the blocks were either very close together or might well be overshadowed by a high warehouse occupying one side of the court. One toilet and one tap in the central yard would probably be the only sanitary provisions and in the early courts built before about 1830 there would be no provision whatsoever and the occupants would have had to rely on cess-pits. Hardly surprising that epidemics of diseases such as cholera, typhoid and smallpox were commonplace.

The areas containing such slums were soon no longer only found within the city centre where incidentally some streets such as Temple Court and Union Court still bear

names reflecting their sordid past. The courts soon spread into the Vauxhall Road and Scotland Road areas in the North and Park Lane, St James Street and the Dingle area in the South. By 1841 a census showed that 56,000 people lived in these courts and a further 20,000 occupied cellars.

Many occupants were waiting to gain a passage on a ship to America and were only temporary residents. Liverpool was the main embarkation port to America for all of Europe and hundreds of thousands passed through the city over the decades. However, thousands, often those in poor health and with no money, were forced to remain here. They were the most vulnerable to the filthy conditions. In 1849 one of the many outbreaks of cholera killed over 5000 people.

It is worth mentioning here that alcohol was another major social problem at this time. in the early 1800's there were no licensing laws and it has been estimated that 1 dwelling house in 7 sold beer. By the 1840s the gin palaces had appeared and there were over 2000 licenced houses in Liverpool selling cheap drink to the working classes. Later in the century pubs became grander, more respectable and were accepted as part of the wider community. Licensing hours, forcing them to close at midnight, were introduced in the 1870s and children were prohibited in 1901. Nonetheless it is hardly surprising that for many a skinful of cheap drink was the obvious escape from their terrible living conditions.

As the slums pushed out over a wider and wider area the wealthy middle classes fled before them. With the development of the early railways travelling became less of a problem and many moved as far out as Mossley Hill, Aigburth and even distant Crosby in the North. Finally the terrible conditions were too disgraceful for the authorities to ignore any longer. In 1846 the Sanitary Act was passed in an attempt to improve housing conditions and Dr Duncan, the country's first Medical Officer of Health was appointed.

From the mid nineteenth century working class housing consisted mainly of terraces built particularly in then almost rural areas such as Everton and Kirkdale. Such houses showed a considerable improvement over the insanitary courts but were still totally unacceptable by today's standards. Some terraces (such as in Arley Street off Vauxhall Road) were little more than front doors opening into single rooms with a central door providing access to the rooms above. From about the 1840s many streets of terraces were built with the backs of houses in two parallel streets being barely separated, either by a very narrow alley or a wall between two tiny back yards. These houses frequently had no windows at the back so that light could only enter at the front, though this was not always as grim as it sounds as there was often only one room per floor. In 1864 an amendment was passed to the earlier Sanitary act to try to improve matters further. 18,000 dwellings (still including 3000 courts) were declared insanitary and the Act empowered the authorities to demolish them. Progress was slow and it took until 1914 for the city to have cleared 10,000, though private enterprise was responsible for some demolition too. About 400 courts were still standing at the outbreak of World War I.

In 1869 the beginning of a revolution in house building occurred with the construction of the country's first municipal housing, St Martin's Cottages in Silvester Street. Although progress was slow here too, with the next major project not undertaken until 1880s when Victoria Square off Scotland Road was built, living conditions improved greatly towards the end of the century. The terraced houses of the late 1800s were usually 2-up, 2 down with back yards and wider passages at the rear. The streets were wider and thus more light reached inside the rooms, probably all of which would by now have had windows. Housing of this type was built quite long distances from the centre of Liverpool spread in a huge fan shape from the centre. Garston, Wavertree and Walton, for example had, and still have, large amounts of housing from this period.

The development of housing in Liverpool during the twentieth century is the personal experience of many of us. The early landing houses have all gone but municipal tenements from the 20s, 30s and 40s are in varying states. Some have been cleared; a few have been renovated and given improved amenities and some of the later ones are still occupied though in desperate need of action. Unfortunately the last 30 years have done little to encourage our faith in local housing policy. The planners in their enthusiasm to improve upon the insanitary conditions, in which thousands were living, chose the indiscriminate use of the bulldozer rather than renovation. Not only were many fine buildings lost but whole communities were shattered. Families and friends were split up removing the network of support and help that existed for all. Worse, the new housing to which people were moved often created more problems for their occupants than the lack of an inside toilet had previously done. The two most unpleasant forms of rehousing from the 1950s on, have been high rise flats and new estates or towns built miles away from the centre. It is now universally acknowledged that high-rise housing was a mistake and many blocks, some less than 20 years old, have been demolished—partly in some cases because the quality of construction and design was so poor. Of the new estates Kirkby is the most famous post war example, though isolated estates such as Speke built in the late 1930s were forerunners of this trend. The concept was that people should be rehoused outside the city in relatively rural surroundings. In fact the residents regarded themselves as having been dumped in a field off the East Lancashire Road. Kirkby's facilities for shopping and entertainments were inadequate and buses into the city were infrequent, expensive and took a long time. Gone was the corner shop, the choice of pubs, the sense of community and, as the nearby industrial estate declined, gone was the chance of local work.

Lessons might have been learnt from experiences at Speke before Kirkby was ever built, for many of the problems were

# The Recent Past

identical. However, the planners did not learn and it has taken a very long time for the mistakes made at Kirkby to be recognised. Many were repeated at Cantril Farm and Netherley, at Cantril Farm the planners even forgot or thought unnecessary, pavements on the estate leaving residents to walk on rough ground or share the roads with the traffic.

It seems that finally attitudes are changing. The emphasis now is on building low density estates much closer to the centre and, at last, renovation has been perceived as a cheaper and more satisfactory alternative to new building. It is tragic that so little is now left to renovate.

It is not only in housing policy that some terrible blunders have been made. Tourism is now widely regarded as one of the main industries for the city's future but we have already destroyed some of our potential tourist attractions.

Many examples of this short sightedness spring to mind. The Overhead Railway, or Docker's Umbrella as it was affectionately nicknamed, ran the length of the docks from Dingle to Seaforth. It was opened in 1893 as the first elevated, electrically operated railway in the world. The 'El' in New York was based on Liverpool's Overhead. When dock traffic declined in the 1950s the railway was closed and dismantled but how marvellous it would be now if some stretches at least had been preserved. The dock estate and dock road area has also lost many fine buildings though at least the finest, The Albert Dock, is being renovated.

The Beatles must be considered the most important tourist attraction of Liverpool today. The history of Beatles' success is known to fans the world over. Guided tours are now conducted around the city showing people where they lived and where Penny Lane can be found. There is one massive gap in this tour—The Cavern Club. I must admit to feeling personally very strongly about the demolition of the Cavern. As a teenager I regularly went there and in February 1966 I attended the closing night when, my brother, Frank's group called 'The Hideaways' who played there a record number of times, were the last to appear. The Cavern re-opened 6 months later with 'The Hideaways' playing again and the event was thought important enough to attract celebrities such as Sir Harold Wilson, Ken Dodd, Jimmy Saville and Bessie Braddock MP. But the halcyon days were over, the now licensed club never recaptured its magic for me. Nonetheless when a foreign tourist gets into my taxi and asks for Mathew Street I can anticipate the look of disgust and disappointment on their face when I explain the Cavern Club was demolished. The new Cavern Walks shopping complex is very fine but it is not what a Japanese fan has come to Liverpool to see. Once again the City has

# Liverpool and Tourism

realised too late the error of its ways. Numerous magnificent pubs; the old heart of the city with its squares; many fine houses—the list is endless—have all been demolished with no thought of either the importance of the past or of the future.

Although everyone in Liverpool habitually refers to 'the dock road', this name does not in fact officially exist. The dock road is merely the common term for a succession of separately named sections of road which run alongside the river to the north and to the south from the city centre. To the north the dock road begins as 'New Quay' at Princes Dock, then changes and becomes Bath Street. The name Bath Street comes from the 18th century sea water baths that were formerly sited here. The baths were demolished in 1817 when Princes Dock was being built. Princes Dock was opened on the coronation of King George IV in July 1821. It was at this period that Liverpool's commerce began to expand on an unprecedented scale. This was when many of the grand brick warehouses were built as the docks spread out from the old city centre transforming the former North Shore. The dock road was rightly famous for its incredible number of pubs, but only about 12 are still standing at the time of writing; we show 2 here. In common with many parts of Britain, precise navigation of the dock road could be achieved via the names, both famous and infamous, of these pubs. One road, Vandries Street, (see photo)

## Off the Dock Road North

was even named after a Dutchman who ran an ancient hostelry on the old North Shore. Further north, the 'dock road' becomes Regent Road as far as Gladstone Dock. Not so long ago this long thoroughfare was bustling with activity but it is now quiet as the docks have gone into decline. The decline of shipping into the Port of Liverpool can be compared to the severing of a main artery. Jobs directly and indirectly linked with the sea were once the life-blood of the City.

Even as late as the 1950's dockers alone numbered approximately 20,000 compared to under 3,000 now. The majority of families in the old parts of Liverpool had men folk working in some capacity at the docks. Going away to sea was a routine occupation for thousands of scousers, and I myself joined the Merchant Navy at the age of 16. Within two decades of my going away to sea, the job of a seaman was almost as extinct as the great liners that once frequented the port. Containerisation and other new technologies are reducing the size of ships crews and there has been a decline in the overall volume of traffic too. The oil

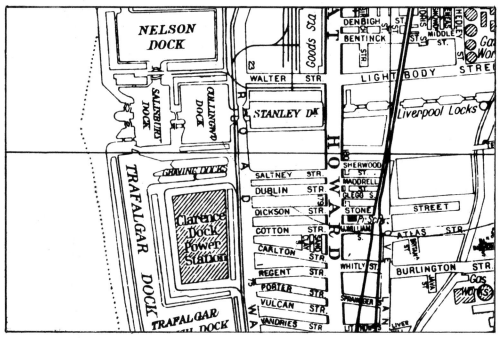

fired ships that I sailed on were a great improvement on their predecessors, the steam ships, upon which an entire culture and way of life was based. Working in the bowels of those steam powered infernos were the fire-men and coal trimmers, many of them from Liverpool, such as my Uncle John Devitt from Scotland Road. My father served in the Royal Navy and together with many others who lived through the war years he told me about the work of these men. All agreed that if there was a harder task involved in any occupation they had not heard of it. The laborious job of the trimmers was to continually fetch coal for the fire-men keeping the boilers fired, in temperatures of up to 130°. Steam Ships and the men who sailed in them are now just a memory in the annals of Liverpool's history, although their association with Liverpool will live on for some time yet.

The continued decline and demolition of Liverpool's waterfront is very evident along Regent Road into Bootle. However, it should not be forgotten that parts of the dockland area have been depopulated for many years not so much because of the bulldozer and the recession but because of the heavy bomb damage during World War 2. Sandhills and Bootle still have much open space and occasionally more modern buildings as a result of wartime bombing.

The Great Howard Street area is an instructive sample of the changed and changing circumstances of the docklands. When St. Augustines Church (see photo) was opened in 1849 Liverpool's already overcrowded slums were still being swelled by poor Irish immigrants. The Church was opened in honour of three Benedictine monks who had died caring for the plague ridden poor who had inhabited this densely populated part of Dock Land. As time passed gradual improvements took place as the slums of the area disappeared, and by the First World War there were only about 3,000 left. The Second World War brought almost total devastation to the area and since then it has become mainly industrial with the residential population virtually nil. Throughout the bombing and demolition the Church itself survived, but with depopulation of the area finally taking its toll, it closed in 1976.

**1** This seven-storey warehouse on Bath Street was demolished in the late 1970's and the former dock road pub 'The International' is now used as a canteen.

**2** Early nineteenth century warehouses on the Bath Street section of the dock road, demolished in the late 1970's.

**3** Early nineteenth century warehouses being demolished in 1967 in Vandries Street, off the Waterloo Road section of the dock road.

**4** The Regent Road section of the north dock road was once a thriving bustling thoroughfare before the dramatic post-war decline of commerce and shipping in Livepool.

**5** Saltney Street off Regent Road, with paved roadway and gas lights, still lit, in 1966. These 'landing' tenements, now demolished, were originally built in 1911 to replace the original infamous slum courts typical of the area.

**6** Stanley dock is the only dock on the landward side of the dock road. The warehouses were built in 1848 by the renowned dock engineer Jesse Hartley who designed the world famous Albert Dock complex south of the city centre.

**7** This tobacco warehouse at Stanley Dock was built in 1900 and is reputed to be the largest warehouse in the world. The massive twelve storey structure of red and blue brick still stands.

**8** The 'American Hotel', Regent Road, at the corner of Blackstone Street was one of the many famous dock road pubs. It was demolished in the 1980's.

**9** Regent Road, in Bootle was the location of this warehouse at Miller's Bridge shown here during demolition in 1984. The crane in the background stands on the edge of Brocklebank Dock. In the background is the "Mammoth" a steam driven floating structure which has worked throughout the docks since 1920. Together with Liverpool's only other floating crane — "Samson" it is to cease working later this year and more than likely demolished.

**10** The small terraced houses in narrow Garden Lane near Park Street, also in Bootle, date from the 1860's and were cleared in 1969.

15

**11** Derby Road, close to Bankhall.

**12** The last block of the old property in Beacon Street at the junction with Boundary Street, was built in the 1830's, this notorious area was known as 'Sebastapol' from the 1850's.

**13** St. Augustines Church, built in 1849, in Great Howard Street.

After the mass demolition of housing in the 1960s, it could be said that the early 1980s was the age of mass demolition of factories. The combined effects of Liverpool's steady decline as a port and the mass unemployment of the current recession is symbolised in the Vauxhall Road area quite simply as the wholesale demolition of factories and warehouses. The dramatic demolition of the huge Tate and Lyle sugar refinery plant in 1983 was taken to be the end of an entire chapter of Liverpool's history. Sugar has been an important part of Liverpool's trade since the seventeenth century. There was a refinery in Liverpool as early as 1670, close to Redcross Street in the city centre. The huge Tate & Lyle plant began its life in the 1870s and operated for over a hundred years. The decline of trade in other commodities, such as tobacco, which were also related to Britain's imperial past has also severely affected Liverpool. Vauxhall Road's reputation as home for an exceedingly large number of pubs is mostly a thing of the past too. Many have been demolished, though it is interesting to note that they are often the last buildings to be cleared on a particular site as breweries are always reluctant to lose licenced premises.

# Off Vauxhall Road

The large number of pubs is a reflection of the density of the population in the nineteenth century. In 1847 Chisenhale Street, only 334 yards long, contained no less than 19 separate courts as well as several early 'landing' blocks. The earliest of these mean courts were given wholly unsuitable, pretty names such as Priscilla Court, Rose Court and Rebecca Court. However, such was the scale of their proliferation that subsequent ones bear only a number or a letter as their identification in the densely populated street.

Typical of the life of the old area was the story told to me many times by my Dad about the old "Lock Fields". Well known in the district years ago, "Lock Fields" was simply a field near Vauxhall Road and the locks of the Leeds-Liverpool canal. When my Dad was a young man this was the place where men would fight each other in the morning, often after an argument in one of the local pubs the night before. The custom was that instead of fighting there and then, they would meet the next morning on the Lock Fields. Hundreds of spectators from the area would be there to watch. Another aspect of old Liverpool now long forgotten.

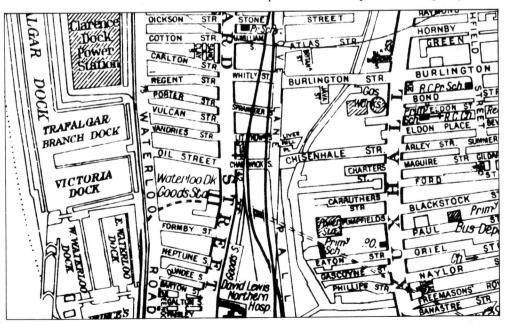

**1** The only building left standing on Chisenhale Street is the public house called the 'Bridge', logically enough perhaps as it stands on the bridge over the famous Leeds and Liverpool canal. Its less prestigious local nickname however is 'The Flyhouse'.

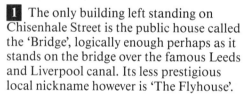

**2** The large, half demolished warehouse which is shown on the right of the photograph adjoined Tate and Lyles. It dated from 1847 but even its listed building status failed to save it.

**3** Seen by many Liverpudlians as a symbol of the destruction of the city's industry during the current recession, the massive Tate and Lyle refinery was undergoing demolition in 1983.

**4** This warehouse dated from 1872 and was also associated with the sugar refining industry which was reaching its peak at that time.

**5** Tiny terraced houses in Arley Street off the eastern side of Vauxhall Road which have long since vanished. There were no windows at all to the rear of this terrace.

**6** 'Scotch Houses' in Arley Street. Note the four doors in a row leading to two upstairs and two downstairs one roomed "bed sitting rooms".

**7** Eldon Place, adjoining Arley Street has another type of dwelling familiar in the old Liverpool slums. The cramped two-up two-down houses with cellars were cleared in the late 1960s along with most of the rest of the area.

**8** The junction of Vauxhall Road and Burlington Street was the site of this warehouse until demolition in 1981. The road was notorious for the large number of pubs it contained, two of which can clearly be seen here.

**9** Burlington Street, off Vauxhall Road, had the characteristic 'landing' houses which were built in many parts of Liverpool in the decade before the First World War to replace the terrible slums of the nineteenth century. They were considered a great improvement at that time and are clearly forerunners of the municipal flats of the inter-war period. This block was demolished in 1970.

**10** Burlington Street also has examples of municipal tenements from different periods. On the left stand flats from the 1920s which are still occupied today. Portland Gardens on the right of the road are from the 1930s and these are undergoing renovation. The chimney of the Tate and Lyle refinery is visible in the background during demolition in 1983.

**11** A typical block of early twentieth century 'landing' houses in St. Silvester Place just prior to demolition in 1966.

**12** This was the first municipal housing in the country, St Martin's Cottages stood in Silvester Street. Erected in 1869 they should surely have been preserved, if not renovated for continued habitation.

**13** Boundary Street at the end of Kirkdale Road is so named because it was the ancient boundary between Liverpool and Kirkdale. These listed Georgian buildings were built around 1830, still standing but in obvious need of repair.

Scotland Road runs along what was once the old coach route to the north from the town centre. But the rural scenery changed dramatically in the nineteenth century as the commerce and industry of a major sea port created workshops, pubs and doss-houses and tens of thousands of poorly built, cramped houses in the narrow streets and courts off the main highway. Its name became—and still is for many people—synonymous with Liverpool, epitomising both the best and the worst, depending on your view point, of the city's attributes. The squalor and strife that existed here from early Victorian times was never quite eradicated. Despite successive waves of demolition and considerable bomb damage during the last war it was still amongst the worst areas of housing in the 1960s. Yet I know I am not alone in believing that here amongst the poor conditions there was as much humour and pride as there was poverty and defeat—just like any working class community in the north. These things are no less true despite having been turned into clichés by being so frequently observed. My memory, certainly, insists that the front door steps glistened from the constant rubbing with sandstone blocks and that

# Around Scottie Road

almost every family boasted at least one 'character' and several natural comedians. I remember one such character, Thomas Gately. A docker for 46 years, he grew up in the mean courts off Scotland Road. He was a distant relative, but to me more like a grand father. Like so many dockland characters he was best known by his nickname. In fact over the years he had two nicknames. Before the war people called him 'The Quiet Man'—because he talked so much! After the war he became known as 'The Lone Ranger', because of his habit of collecting pieces of silver paper. He amassed sacks full over the years to raise money for charity. 'Gate' as he was known to his close friends was full of odd comic rhymes and sayings. Amongst my most abiding memory of Gate was, if I was ever a 1d or 2d short for the pictures (which was sometimes funded by taking back empty jam jars for 1d refund). He would always give me the coppers saying his immortal line "Come back when yer 21".

The Scottie Road area is full of such memories for me for I was born on

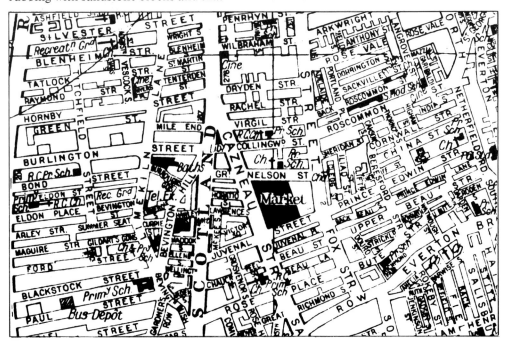

Hopwood Street just off Scotland Road. These streets were our playground until we moved in the 1950s.

My brothers and I spent much of our childhood in the streets and alleys of the district. One of our favourite games in those days was to turn one of the old gas lamps into a swing. We would sway about wildly hanging onto an old car tyre suspended from a rope lashed to the cross bar.

During the 1960s, the whole Scotland Road area began to change beyond recognition particularly with the building of the second Mersey Tunnel. Scottie Road itself has been greatly reduced. The frontage has completely disappeared from the start of Byrom Street to the original Mersey Tunnel with just the section from the tunnel northward to the Rotunda remaining of this once notorious hub of old Liverpool. The Rotunda was a former theatre that stood at the junction of Scotland Road and Stanley Road and the name is still commonly used for this junction.

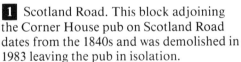
**1** Scotland Road. This block adjoining the Corner House pub on Scotland Road dates from the 1840s and was demolished in 1983 leaving the pub in isolation.

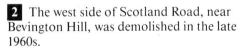
**2** The west side of Scotland Road, near Bevington Hill, was demolished in the late 1960s.

**3** The 'Westmoreland Arms' Scotland Road, known locally as the 'Honky Tonk' bears an inscription which reads "One of Liverpool's oldest pubs established in 1740". The adjoining block has since been renovated. In the background stands Woodstock Gardens awaiting demolition.

**4** Ashfield Gardens off the western side of Scotland Road awaiting demolition in 1983.

**5** Woodstock Gardens were typical pre-war municipal flats, shown here awaiting demolition in 1983. Visible through the arch is St Anthony's Church, Scotland Road, built in 1833.

**6** 'The Ship', established in 1858, was at the corner of Latimer Street and Hopwood Street and was still open for business in 1983 when it was gutted by fire.

**7** 'The Globe' another of Scottie Roads old pubs, at the corner of Woodstock Street was closed in 1969 and demolished soon after.

**8** and **9** These 'landing' houses in Hornby Street were built in the early 1900s to replace older slums; they were themselves demolished at the end of the 1960s.

**10** An old block of houses including a former stable on Limekiln Lane at the corner of Tatlock Street. The League of Welldoers Club now occupies this site.

**11** Three storey houses undergoing demolition on Norris Street in 1967, the central door provided the entrance to the inner court.

**12** and **13** Louis Street and Taliesen Street off the eastern side of Scotland Road were typical streets of the area. The 3 storey houses in Taliesen Street had no rear windows at all.

**14** Victoria Square, built in the 1880s was an ambitious scheme to replace the horrific slums of the nineteenth century. The five storey tenement blocks contained 282 flats and won an architectural award for their advanced design when first erected. The photograph shows its demolition in 1966.

Stanley Road in Kirkdale is the long major road which runs from the Rotunda at Scotland Road northwards into Bootle. Before it reaches Bootle it passes through the heart of Kirkdale. This was my dad's old neighbourhood, he was born in Blackfield Street. This area holds many memories from my childhood when I used to visit my Auntie Kath in Lambeth Road. Despite warnings I would sneak down notorious Reading Street and watch the gangs of men playing cards behind the tenements. These card games were known as "toss schools" and were an important, though usually secretive, form of entertainment for many men in the pre-television era of the 1950's. To get to Auntie Kath's I used to catch a tram from Sleeper's Hill to Lambeth Road. Sleeper's Hill was also the starting point for our gang when we travelled on a tram, perhaps to the "distant" country at Kirkby Woods. The adventure of trams was never quite maintained when they were replaced by buses in 1956. Nevertheless a ride on a new bus to far off places such as Otterspool was still magical. It always seems such a shame that the variety of colours of the buses, yellow in Wallasey or blue in Birkenhead, has gone and a uniform green

## Kirkdale across to Walton

is the order of today. The operation of the buses has also been transformed since those days. I drove a bus myself for seven years when the full 'crew' included a conductor and when the job was more interesting and often hilarious. Many of the conductors were jovial and helpful to their passengers but sadly this personal aspect of the job diminished greatly when they were replaced by today's driver-only operation.

But Stanley Park, on the border of Anfield, holds the key to the warmest recollections, where with countless other children I would spend hours playing during the Summer months. The tiny row of shops shown in the photograph in this section was directly opposite the swings in the park. When we had money (usually a penny) we would go over there for an incredible choice of riches—a lolly ice, a penny 'Vantas' drink or, a favourite in those days, an 'Arrow' bar. Alongside the park swings was the 'show', a wooden shed with a raised stage. From time to time a clown, ventriloquist or similar act would appear and a large queue of kids would be waiting with their threepenny

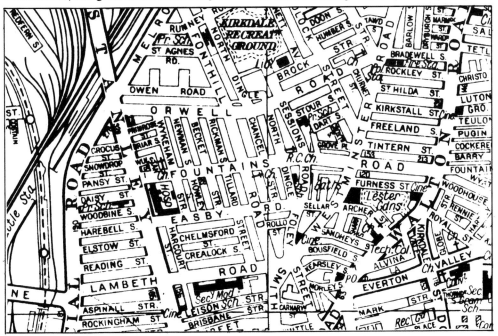

Joey's to get in. For those with no money there were always the trees for the grandstand view. The children themselves often got up on the stage and I remember one day in 1958 my brother Frank got up on stage and sang an Everley Brother's song to tremendous applause, (my older brother Jackie and our gang had 'persuaded' the other children to clap for our Frank). Stanley Park was the first park in Liverpool to have an open air swimming bath and it was extremely popular. At times there would be droves of us from the streets in our neighbourhood around Blessington Road converging on the baths with our bottles of water and 'jam butties'. Sadly the baths and the 'show' no longer exist. They are now just a wonderful memory. Gone too are the rowing boats. The little hut where we would pay sixpence to hire a boat is still standing but it is extensively vandalised. The only other reminder is the small jetty where the boats were tied up.

**1** This substantial, well constructed block on Stanley Road at the junction with Lambeth Road, shows the red engineering brick characteristic of much of this area.

**2** Brighton Terrace in Stanley Road was unusual for its elevated position, now demolished.

**3** Flinders Street, off Commercial Road, was typical of a great number of terraces built from the 1860's. The site is now a football pitch and all of the surrounding streets have been cleared. This part of Kirkdale is presently a wilderness and post-war housing too is being demolished.

**4** Reading Street became a notorious street in Liverpool with some of the earliest of the tenement buildings dating from the mid nineteenth century. The last sections were not finally cleared until the early 1960's, many of the former residents being rehoused in Kirkby.

**5** Elstow Street, adjoining Reading Street, contained very poor terraced housing, by the time it was demolished in 1977. 'Tillotsons' factory, visible in the background on Commercial Road, is now derelict.

**6** Great Mersey Street, off Stanley Road was one of the early streets of rural Kirkdale village. At the junction with Smith Street stood a Victorian pub, 'The Britannia' flanked on both sides by earlier housing. Virtually all this block was demolished in the early 70's.

**7** Blackfield Street. These early nineteenth century terraces with front gardens would have been on the very edge of town and much sought after when first built. The once attractive street has been replaced by a new housing development.

**8** Brisbane Street, off Smith Street, illustrates another type of two storey terrace. The special features of these small houses was that they had windows at the rear on the upper floor only.

**9** Seen here from Latham Street, a rear view of the unusual construction of the terraced houses in Brisbane Street.

**10** 3 storey mid-Victorian terraced in Vesuvius Street, shown here in dereliction in 1966.

**11** Another variation on a familiar theme, this 'landing' house block in Smith Street had central stairs for access to the upper floors. The building faced Whittle Street which itself contained many similar ones dating from the 1890's.

**12** At the junction of Smith Street and Kirkdale Road stood this massive well-built public house with interesting decorative brickwork. The site of the 'Goats Head' is now landscaped.

**13** Westminster Road Baths are still standing although the original frontage of 1876 was demolished along with many other adjacent properties when a new road scheme, now abandoned, was planned for this once busy main thoroughfare.

**14** This small block of back-to-back houses, Church Terrace, stood in Archer Street, off Westminster Road. It was opposite St Mary's Church which was built in 1835. The terrace and the church—once a part of rural Kirkdale before the adjoining industrial city overran it—were demolished in the early 1970's.

**15** This early Victorian terrace was situated in the gentle curve of Sessions Road—aptly named as it originally lead to old Kirkdale gaol, around 1819. This photograph from 1967 shows the houses in considerable decay.

**16** A pub bearing the old name 'The Elm Tree' stands on this site, but not the one shown here which was demolished in 1978. The site at Westminster Road and Barlow Lane junction is believed to be an ancient one of many former inns. This junction is that of the original lanes which led to the old villages of Walton and Bootle.

**17** Small, mid-Victorian terraced houses of four rooms plus cellars stood in Whitefield Lane. This narrow lane is now part of the site of a housing estate built in the late 1970's. The immediate vicinity of Westminster Road contained some fine Victorian houses alongside these poor terraces.

**18** Fonthill House, Melrose Road was one of four tenement blocks built in 1923. These were demolished in 1983 whilst identical blocks of the same period still stand in the Dingle, south of the city.

**19** This unusual block of terraced houses built above a row of tiny shops stood on Walton Lane opposite Stanley Park. This scene is from 1964.

**20** This substantial Victorian terrace at the junction of Walton Lane and Alexander Square should surely have been renovated. New housing now stands here following demolition of the original buildings in the early 1970's.

**21** Walton Road, formerly one of Liverpool's main shopping districts is now sad and desolate.

**22** Walton Road boasted many fine pubs. One recent sad closure was the Penrhyn Castle.

**23** Stanley Park lake with the jetty and boat hiring hut, sadly no longer in use.

Massive and often indiscriminate housing clearance characterises the last 25 years of this district. Once again potentially fine, solid buildings were destroyed at the same time as the mean slums which richly deserved their fate. Unfortunately little is left to remind us of the interesting history of the area for few buildings have benefitted from renovation. It is impossible to imagine now the rural village of Everton to which the middle classes began to move in the late eighteenth century in search of the peace of the country. High rise flats now dominate the ridge which was once covered with teeming terraced streets and when St George's Church and Our Lady Immaculate school were the tallest buildings. In more recent years policy makers have built housing estates rather than the multi storey flats which were once favoured by planners—if not the people who lived in them. In fact some tower blocks dating from the 1950's and 60's are already being demolished. We certainly do not build to last in the way our predecessors did.

Two horrendous examples of modern housing are found here: the Piggeries and Radcliffe Estate. The Piggeries, which have not been honoured with a photograph, are

## Around Everton

to be found off Everton Brow. The name is given to three blocks of high rise flats built in the 1960's which now stand empty despite suggestions for both demolition and renovation. The Radcliffe Estate dating from the mid 1970's also has an undecided future. Photograph 38 gives a pretty clear idea of existing conditions. The estate was a planning and architectural disaster and the sooner it is demolished the better. The widespread demolition in this district has meant the break up of many old communities but for once this is not entirely to be mourned. Religious divisions had been rife with Catholics and Protestants tending to live within specific areas. Catholics were mainly found around Scotland Road while Protestants lived in the Netherfield Road area. Serious riots and fighting had been regular occurrences on St Patrick's Day and the 12th of July but as the areas were cleared and the communities dispersed from the 1950's such incidents have, fortunately, been much less frequent.

Our family moved in the early 1950s to a terraced house off Blessington Road, in the

nearby Anfield district where my brothers, sister, and I spent the rest of our childhood. Like many Liverpool kids football was one of our major activities and the cobbled surface of Blessington Road was often our pitch. It seems to me now that we rarely saw a car, for the match could go on for hours disturbed only by our parents finally calling us into the house. Among the kids of the neighbourhood playing football was Kenny, younger brother of a well known scouser, Liverpool entertainer Johnny Kennedy. Others of the old gang were Frank Darcy who later went on to play for Everton and our next door neighbour in Gurnall Street, Alan Banks, who later played for Liverpool!

**1** The once thriving district off Great Homer Street was reputed to be the busiest shopping area outside the city centre until the mid 1960's.
In 1964 the new shopping precinct was being constructed when this photo was taken. So many people have been rehoused that the area is now a shadow of its former self.

**2** The area between Great Homer Street and Everton Ridge once contained some of Liverpool's worst housing conditions as in Adelaide Place photographed during demolition in the mid 1960's.

**3** The Wynstay pub, at the corner of Portland Place and Roscommon Street, was derelict in 1979. Happily this fine building has been completely renovated and re-opened as a pub once more. It is now named 'The Cotton Picker'.

**4**

**5**

**4** and **5** The front and back of Carson Street are shown here. These 3 storey houses had no rear windows and would have had tiny backyards containing the taps for the occupants' water supply. The houses date from about 1840 and were demolished in 1964.

**6** and **7** Thorneycliffe Street also shows early housing which must have been somewhat dark inside as only the front had windows.

**8** Ellison Street and Luther Street showing some of Liverpool's true back-to-back houses being demolished in 1965.

**9** These houses in Elias Street are another variation on the theme of poor terraced housing in this district. They have no back doors and the outside toilets were on the upper level between the very small yards.

**10** The Ann Fowler Salvation Home for Women on Netherfield Road South was a well known local landmark. This imposing listed building was originally built as a Welsh Independent Chapel in 1867. It operated as a hostel until 1983 but was sadly set on fire by vandals after its closure and has had to be demolished.

**11** Cresswell Mount was built in 1956 and was Liverpool's first completed multi-storey block. It stood at the top of St George's Hill prior to demolition in 1984.

**12** Many of the streets on the slopes of Everton Ridge were extremely steep and had hand rails on the pavements to help pedestrians. The housing dates from the middle of the last century. Nicholson Street in 1968 is shown here.

**13** This photograph shows the rear of the two-up, two-down houses in Patmos Street and, beyond them, Our Lady Immaculate School which I attended. The school was built in the 1880s and demolished in the early 1970s.

**14** Cicero Terrace, running parallel to Northumberland Terrace, was typical of the average standard of housing in the area.

**15** Northumberland Terrace at the top of the ridge would have had fine views over the city and Mersey. These mid Victorian houses are obviously much grander than those on the slopes below and would have been built for middle class families.

**16** and **17** York Terrace, at the end of Northumberland Terrace, also contained some splendid dwellings. The particularly high block at the corner of Hobart Street would have had steep flights of steps to give access to the raised front doors.

**18** This substantial Victorian terrace stood in Everton Valley. Its grand proportions are made even more imposing by its commanding height above stone steps leading to gateways. One of these houses was the home of John Shell, a member of "The Hideaways". Tragically John, who was born in Dallas though he had always lived in Liverpool, was drafted into the US Army and was killed in Vietnam. Many will remember his funeral, with full military honours, held in Anfield.

**19** At the bottom of Everton Valley stood this magnificent, Victorian ornately tiled public house. 'The Derby Arms'.

**20** The Church of Our Lady Immaculate on St Domingo Road was designed by Pugin and built in 1856 as the Lady Chapel and Chancel Chapels for a proposed Roman Catholic Cathedral which was never built. The chapel instead became, and remains, the Parish church and is a listed building. The municipal tenements on the right are Sir Thomas White Gardens which were demolished in 1984.

**21** The top of St Domingo Road is one of the highest points in Liverpool and was used as the site for a beacon from, perhaps, the thirteenth century. St George's Church, another listed building, now occupies the site. Our photograph shows nearby Beacon Lane, this large building, also by Pugin, was built in 1861 and started life as an orphanage, became a munitions factory during World War II and finally a furniture factory before it was pulled down in 1969.

**22** The Liver pub, known as Fitzy's, was another well known landmark at the junction of Beacon Lane and Robson Street until it disappeared in the early 1970's. This photograph and the following 4 are streets on the border between Anfield and Everton.

40

**23** Sleepers Hill is named after the common land that existed in the area known as 'Great & Little Sleeper'. Fortunately not all the houses off Sleepers Hill are being demolished, some are being renovated. The Stanley pub was opened in 1891 and is still open. The new housing in the background is on the site of the Liver (Photo 22).

**24** Our old cobbled 'football pitch' of Blessington Road as it was in 1965.

**25** Only part of Burleigh Road South is still standing and has now been renovated. This portion and St Cuthbert's Church were demolished in 1970.

**26** The demolition of these terraces on Towson Street should not be mourned. They were a mixture of 2 and 3 storey cellar dwellings providing poor accommodation. Anfield, home of Liverpool Football Club, can be seen in the distance.

**27**

**2**

**28**

**3**

**29**

**27** In 1973 Desmond Street off Heyworth Street which is the continuation of St. Domingo Road, was quite rightly demolished, with it went another church, St Benedicts.

**28** Friar Street was another typical street from the 1860-80 period. It is now open grassland but new housing is scheduled for the land.

**29** The streets off the western side of Heyworth Street were built 10-20 years earlier and were also of poor quality. This is Samuel Street and the back of Priory Road in 1966.

**30** and **31** Druid Street and Waterhouse Street were of similar style to those shown above. The latter were especially mean with no back doors and tiny yards. The beginning of Waterhouse Street can now be traced by the street sign on the side of The Thistle public house but it only runs a few yards before petering out at the edge of the Everton Park development.

**32** and **33** These 4 roomed houses in Sampson Street were built below street level and the road itself was never even properly surfaced. As the rear view shows these houses also lacked back doors.

**34** These substantial houses stood in Eastbourne Street until the large scale clearance of the 1960's. They were built for the Victorian middle classes and had elegant doorways and wrought iron balconies and railings. Fortunately, a similar terrace from 1824 on Everton Road has been saved and is being renovated.

**35** Working class housing later surrounded Eastbourne Street. This photograph shows the rear of Village Grove situated behind the fine terrace above. The house frontages are not unusual but the back yards were completely enclosed by these high walls.

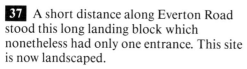

**36** Rupert Lane was named after Prince Rupert who was the Royalist general who took Liverpool during the Civil War. He placed his headquarters on nearby Everton Brow in 1644. These three storey terraces came down in 1968.

**37** A short distance along Everton Road stood this long landing block which nonetheless had only one entrance. This site is now landscaped.

**38** The Radcliffe Estate off Everton Road dating from the mid 1970's is a classic example of failure by planners and architects. It was originally designed as an echo of a Cornish village; instead it was a maze of dark passages and complicated walkways.

**39** The appropriately named Castle pub stood on the corner of Tynemouth Street and was left in splendid isolation when photographed in 1974.

**40** Newlands Street off Breck Road was named after James Newlands, Liverpool's first borough engineer. This terrace is of 3 storey houses though, as the photograph shows, the attic floors generally have no front windows, only skylights.

**41** Another typical street was Fishguard Street shown here in 1967 when half demolished although some houses were obviously still occupied. This street was the birthplace in 1902, of Paul McCartney's father, James. The family also lived elsewhere in Everton including Solva Street and Lloyd Street both shown below. Their next home was Sir Thomas White Gardens followed by furnished rooms in Anfield where Paul was born.

**42** Solva Street was very similar except it still retained its cobbled road probably because it was a cul-de-sac and was still unadopted in 1967.

**43** There can be little doubt that Lloyd Street, off Everton Road, had to be demolished. The subsidence of these houses is only too evident.

**44** Much grander houses stood in St Chrysostum Street but this did not save them. They too came down in the 1960's. How much better it would have been to renovate these elegant Victorian houses than to build the Queens Road Estate.

**45** This housing in Back Phoebe Anne Street has to be amongst the meanest still standing in Liverpool in 1966. The houses were back-to-backs and note how few windows there are—economy housing of the early Victorian period.

**46** This view of the Spencer Street area shows how complete areas were cleared. Only the tower of Everton Water Works, built in 1853 by Liverpool's first Water Engineer, Thomas Duncan, now still survives.

**47** Larch Grove stood off Larch Lea where Liverpool's Evertonian personality Billy Butler grew up. The factory is Barker and Dobsons, still a thriving sweet manufacturers when photographed in 1968. Today this factory is due for demolition. Note the fine cast iron street light.

Islington runs east from the grand suite of municipal buildings that stands on St John's Plateau overlooking the city. Today, sadly, the grandeur of Liverpool ends where Islington begins. The complete frontage of the street has disappeared in the path of a new road scheme, though it must be admitted that many of the buildings had already fallen into disrepair.

The whole area around Islington has been in a state of flux for some years now. The prime causes have been twofold: the building of the new Royal Liverpool Hospital complex swallowed large amounts of land and major road building schemes have cut huge swathes through the district. These were connected with the completion of the Wallasey tunnel under the Mersey and the need to improve commuter routes to the city. Large numbers of houses have been cleared and shops in the area now struggle for survival. Most recent building has been for industrial and commercial uses in an attempt to bring work back to the area.

It is ironic that in the late eighteenth and early nineteenth century this locality was a well off, middle class area. St Anne Street, named after the church which stood here, even had genteel sports facilities: an archery

# From Islington to Edge Hill

range, a bowling green and a tennis court. However, the city was then expanding so rapidly that all this would have been swallowed up soon after the turn of the century by working class housing such as courts and low quality terraces. From later periods this area also had several interesting examples of landing block and some are shown below.

In Edge Hill part of the old village centre fortunately still stands around Mount Vernon Road and Holland Place and some buildings are now being renovated. The hill on which stood the Lybro factory, (Photo 22) is one of the highest points in South Lancashire and in 1886 was the site for the Liverpool Shipperies Exhibition. For this large commercial exhibition a replica of the Eddystone lighthouse, over 130 feet high, was erected. The light could be seen for 40 miles and the view from the top must have been magnificent. There is still a pub in Durning Road called the Shipperies which commemorates this exhibition but nothing else remains.

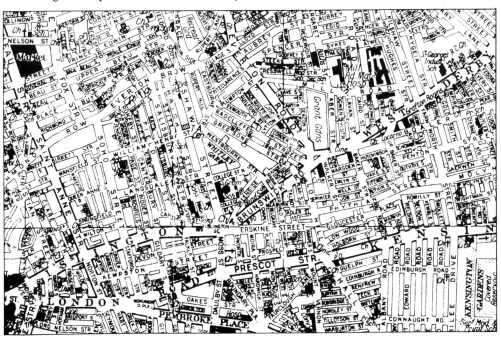

 St Anne Street police station now stands on the site of this 'landing' block. This is a relatively late example dating from just before the First World War.

 This large tenement block was built in 1923 when the old court dwellings were being cleared. It stood on Holly Street off St Anne Street.

 Close to Mansfield Street stands a building erected for a carriage hire business in 1876. It still carries an inscription, not showing here, which advertises 'Wedding Equipages, Broughams, Phaetons, Private Omnibuses, Waggonettes and Funeral Carriages and all other requisites'. It also claims 'Appointments of a Superior Description'. Presumably this was the home of the forerunner of today's car hire business.

**4** and **5** Richmond Row running into Fox Street is the site of this dilapidated hotch-potch of buildings which is surprisingly still standing at the time of writing. It is obviously many years since the upper stories were used. Richmond Row was the original route between Everton and the city centre.

**6** The Soho Street area now seems to have an air of despair with particularly high unemployment locally. These grim municipal tenements known locally as the Four Squares did nothing to improve the environment and were demolished in 1977.

**7** The Great Eastern pub on Langsdale Street survived the clearance of the rest of the area. Regrettably it closed in 1983 making the future of this impressive building uncertain.

**8** Kempston Street was once the home of Frankie Vaughan. These 'landing' houses dating from 1902 had side flights of stairs and landings at the rear. This area is now designated for commercial and industrial usages.

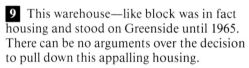

**9** This warehouse—like block was in fact housing and stood on Greenside until 1965. There can be no arguments over the decision to pull down this appalling housing.

**10** Nearby Back College Street also provided very poor conditions and deserved to be condemned. The back of this terrace was just a long blank wall containing no windows at all.

**11** There are very few of these raised terraces left today though in the 1960s they were still quite common. Talbot Street shown here was demolished in the late 1960s. Yates Street and Corn Street in the Dingle provide surviving examples.

**12** The Blue Ball pub was named with reference to the police station next door to it on Prescot Street. The Royal Liverpool Hospital now occupies virtually all one side of the street which was demolished in 1977 to make way for the hospital.

**13** Gloucester Place off Low Hill contained this later 'landing' block with the landing at a higher level and dormer windows to light the attics. Unlike the others shown here the landing is not over shops but more houses, thus built one on top of the other.

**14** This 'landing' block stood behind the Hippodrome Cinema on Winter Street. Here, the stairs to this shorter block are at one end.

**15** The houses on the left hand side of Rockwood Street which stood near Farnworth Street were obviously the posh ones with bay windows, cellars and an attic floor in some.

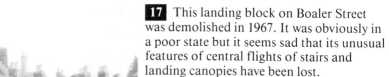

**16** This lamp standard in Fedora Street off West Derby Road had not been treated with much respect. This terrace had the uncommon feature of a tiled canopy over the ground floor windows.

**17** This landing block on Boaler Street was demolished in 1967. It was obviously in a poor state but it seems sad that its unusual features of central flights of stairs and landing canopies have been lost.

**18** The Sacred Heart Church on Hall Lane can be seen in the background of this photograph of Ambrose Street. The houses have long gone and a new road scheme may mean the end for the church too.

**19** Tillotson Street off Hall Street had 3 storey terraces which unusually had no cellars.

**20** and **21**  The Royal Liverpool
Hospital occupies the site of Bengal Street.
It is interesting to note, in the rear shot, that
the terraces in the foreground have no back
windows whilst the rest of the street did.
The corner of the Vernon Arms pub is just
visible.

**22**  In the early nineteenth century
"Vernon's Hall" stood here and from this
Mount Vernon was named. The Lybro
Factory was a well known landmark until its
demolition in 1983. The tower to the right is
that of St Mary's Church, one of the earliest
city churches built in 1812.

**23**  Albert Terrace, off Queensland Street,
was a block with three storeys at the front
sloping to two at the back. This terrace was
demolished in the 1960s and new housing
built in the area; this too is now being
demolished.

**24** This row of shops had very small flats rather than houses over it. It stood at the top of Smithdown Lane until 1968.

**25** Bamber Street nearby had poor housing which deserved demolition. These streets were dominated by the large chimney which was a ventilation chimney for the early railway.

The Toxteth district grew at the end of the 18th and beginning of the 19th centuries as one of the fashionable parts of Liverpool in which wealthy merchants established themselves amongst parks at the edge of the old city. For centuries old Liverpool was bounded by Toxteth Park and the villages of West Derby, Everton and Kirkdale. Toxteth Park was actually a royal forest which was 'disparked' in 1591 and the township of Toxteth was established in 1640. Its absorption into the suburbs of Liverpool came with the growth of Liverpool's prosperity and the housing aspirations of the city's wealthy during the 1800s. Toxteth today still has many fine Georgian and early Victorian houses, although a vast number of original ones were allowed to decay and have vanished. As recently as the 1970s entire streets and terraces were demolished, noticeably in the area around the University as the campus expanded into the Grove Street and Myrtle Street region. Other principal roads, squares and boulevards suffered major losses and only in the last few years have attempts been made to restore and renovate what remains. Upper Parliament Street might be seen as an example of this 'eleventh hour' shift of

# The Upper Parliament Street Area

policy.

Upper Parliament Street was laid out on the old boundary between Liverpool and Toxteth and runs eastwards from the river and the old 18th century city. This route begins near the river as Parliament Street, named in 1773, as part of what was then the new township of Harrington. Parliament Street had been known, appropriately enough as 'Townsend Lane' prior to this date. The name 'Harrington' gradually disappeared as Liverpool expanded and the Toxteth district rapidly developed during the late eighteenth and early 19th century. In the eastern parts of this growing district elegant squares and substantial terraces were established. On present day Grove Street stands a recently renovated block of Georgian dwellings which makes up a section of Falkner Square, one of the few remaining squares in Liverpool. On either side of this block now stands new housing where until the 1960s stood Georgian houses similar to those still in evidence on the opposite side of Grove Street. Most of

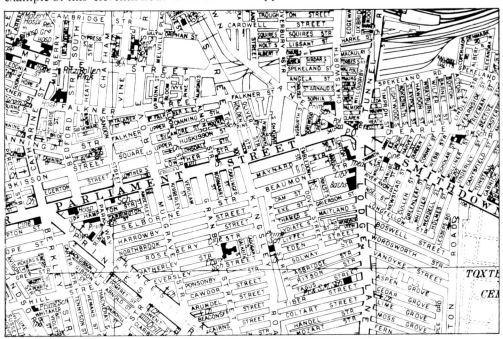

Abercrombie Square off Oxford Street—a particularly splendid example—has survived as part of the University accommodation. Behind the elegant squares, along narrower streets and alleys off the broader roads and boulevards, numerous more humble dwellings were built. Examples of this aspect of Toxteth can be seen in the photographs—Mona Street and Bloom Street behind the more fashionable and prominent Myrtle Street and on narrow Florist Street lying behind the grander Grove Street and Crown Street. Many other earlier and often smaller terraced houses had long been regarded as slums, yet handsome good quality housing—much of it late Georgian—has been unnecessarily cleared along with the sub-standard and derelict.

An obvious example of the poorer cramped housing from the 1860s was Aigburth Street (see photo) in the area at the very top of Upper Parliament Street. The original infamous slums of this area, especially further towards Smithdown Lane, dated from the 1830s and much of this was not cleared until the 1930s. This district was particularly badly over crowded and squalid during the 1830s. Barton Lane, which ran where Entwistle Heights now stands, had 5 unnamed courts though it was only 80 yards long. This was probably the largest area of slum housing outside the city boundary at that time. Yet the 'slum clearance' programmes of the sixties produced very dubious results, as 'high rise' blocks took over from the terraced streets. Entwistle Heights (in photo with Milner House) was the highest of the multi-storey flats when it was opened in 1964. Twenty years later this and many similar flats are due for demolition. Others have already been taken down!

Opinions will probably always differ as to precisely which houses and streets were best demolished and which should have been preserved. But surely the type represented by Longsdale Street (see photo) for example has never been replaced by anything remotely comparable in quality or appeal? Leaving aside the question of the much despised tower blocks, even the new houses that stand on the cleared sites of many of Toxteth's former streets would not bear comparison to the original ones had they been renovated. The wisdom of so much of the re-development in the fifties and sixties is certainly questionable when we see—as the photo of Upper Hill Street shows—the new, some twenty years on, being demolished alongside the old.

1 Cumberland Terrace, Upper Parliament Street was built in 1847 and was demolished in 1978 whilst neighbouring blocks were being renovated.

2 On Upper Parliament Street at the corner of Park Way, the unique 'Stanley House' still stands semi-derelict.

**3** Upper Parliament Street, a listed
building and a splendid example of the
Georgian houses that were typical of the
area. It was demolished in the 1980's to
make way for the inner ring road.

**4** A Mid-Victorian terrace which stood in
Crown Street until the 1960's. This section
of the street has now been completely
cleared and 'landscaped'.

**5** Myrtle Street from the corner of Vine
Street. The municipal flats standing beyond
the junction with Grove Street have survived
whilst similar ones have been demolished.
These flats have been renovated and sold by
a private developer.

**6** Bloom Street, off Myrtle Street,
showing modest but well-built terraces with
cellars and small front gardens.

**7**

**8**

**9**

**1(**

**7** Mona Street off Myrtle Street in an advanced state of decay in the 1960's.

**8** This once-elegant terrace of three-storey houses with basements stood in Vine Street until the late 1960's. The entire street has since been cleared and is now part of the University campus.

**9** Large Georgian houses in Grove Street at the junction with Falkner Street.

**10** Three-storey terraced houses, cramped dwellings with no rear windows, standing on old Florist Street which ran between Grove Street and Crown Street. Cleared in 1967, only the 'Oxford' pub remains.

58

**11** Lonsdale Street, shown here in 1969. These modest terraces had many fine features and very few examples of these well-built houses survive today. St Nathaniel's church, seen in the background, dates from the 1860s and still stands today amidst new housing.

**12** Elegant Georgian houses in Upper Huskisson Street, like too many others they never survived the 1960s.

**13** Aigburth Street, typical of the poorer housing at the top of elegant Upper Parliament Street. Photographed in 1967, Milner House flats are being constructed on the cleared site, with Entwistle Heights which opened in 1965 towering in the background. Both blocks are now due for demolition.

**14** Exe Street, typical of the nineteenth century two-up two-down terraced houses cleared from many parts of the city in the 1960s. Many similar properties survive still, particularly in the Lodge Lane area.

**15** Beaumont Street, off Lodge Lane, in an area of Toxteth which was once known as 'Windsor'. These mid-Victorian houses were demolished in 1969 to make way for new housing.

**16** Many Victorian houses built in the 1870s survive in various states of repair in Princes Road. The prestigious residential boulevard was originally laid out in 1846 to run from Upper Parliament Street southwards to Princes Park. It is interesting to note that this dual carriageway has two names: the southbound road is Princes Avenue while the northbound is Princes Road.

**17** Vronhill Street, off High Park Street was cleared in the early 1980s.

**18** A scene which sums up much about the modern inner city, evoking for many people a mixture of sadness, nostalgia and anger. The last survivor of the original buildings on Upper Hill Street, another old local—The Grecian—stands closed whilst the sub-standard flats and houses which surround it are being demolished after only twenty years service.

**19** 'Stanhope Cottages' (1902) in Upper Stanhope Street were demolished in the late 1960s.

**20** The David Lewis Building was another fine building demolished during the building of the inner ring road. It stood at St Georges Place between St James Place and Great George Street.

**21** These larger Georgian houses on St James Road, shown here from the rear, were demolished in the late 1960s along with the poorer, cramped two-storey terraces lower down the slope on the river side of the Anglican Cathedral.

**22** Sands Street South in the shadow of the Anglican Cathedral towering above on the slope running down to Great George Street.

The Dingle area of Liverpool is South of the city centre, close to the once thriving South docks complex. This location has meant that over the years the Dingle has provided living accommodation for many people working in dock related industries. Examples of several types of early municipal housing can be found here. Many were occupied until the 1960s but most have fortunately now been demolished. Ironically it is some of the earliest housing here, such as the terrace shown in Dingle Lane which seems most likely to survive. This terrace would have been luxurious compared with the 'courts' that pre-existed it. The same can be said of virtually all the examples shown here even though they were of a poor standard by 1960s expectations. Recently the emphasis has been on landscaping derelict land and building low density housing. The riverside International Garden Festival, 1984 site borders onto Dingle and provides a splendid example of creative reclamation of a totally derelict and polluted stretch of land.

# Dingle

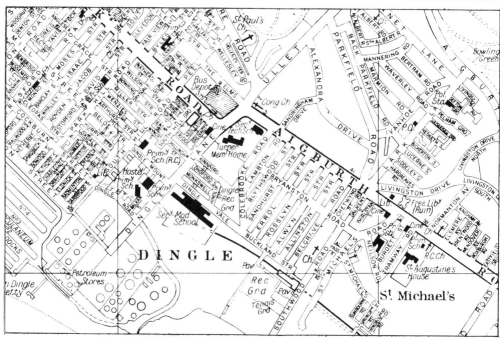

**1** Dingle Lane runs from the end of Park Road towards the Mersey and provides an excellent example of worthwhile renovation. The terrace is early for the area as the plaque set into the sandstone wall indicates, it reads: Borough of Liverpool, erected by the Health Committee 1865.

**2** and **3** These 2 tenement blocks at the Aigburth end of Park Road date from 1923 when they were considered to be fine housing. Both Dingle House and South Hill House are currently scheduled for demolition.

**4** This view of the Dingle tenements shows clearly their proximity to the International Garden Festival site.

**5** Close by these tenements is Dingle Mount, a block of walk-up flats built in the 1930s but nearing the end of its life.

**6** South Street ran from Princes Gate at the entrance to Princes Park to Park Road in the Dingle. This section of handsome mid-Victorian houses with gardens at the Park Road end of South Street disappeared in 1966.

**7** These substantial 3 storey terraces in Harlow Street were demolished in the 1960s although it has taken until the mid 1980s for replacement housing to be built.

**8** A general view of the Pecksniff and Micawber Street area; streets near Park Road named after Dickens' characters. This poor housing, long overdue for demolition, finally went in the early 1980s.

**9** This 'landing' house was built in 1913 and lasted until the late 1960s. It stood in Northumberland Street which runs between Windsor Street and Sefton Street.

**10** Warwick Gardens tenement block was one of the many municipal blocks of flats in the Dingle area. It stood at the junction of Caryl Street and Warwick Street.

**11** A lone Georgian house standing in Stanhope Street shortly before demolition.

**12** Beaufort Street, off Stanhope Street, grim, far from elegant, terraced houses.

The proximity of this area to the city centre and Liverpool's earliest docks made it, in the past, one of the city's most busy and prosperous areas. Regrettably, this is difficult to imagine from its appearance today. Even more regrettable is that so much of the area's decline and demolition has occurred within the last 25 years.

Liverpool's original harbour known as the Pool was fed by a creek which ran along the line of Whitechapel and Paradise Street. Although plans for a dock had been considered as early as 1561 it was not until 1715 that the conversion of the Pool into the Old Dock was completed. This dock was filled in 1826 and its site is now occupied by the Canning Place block. Canning Dock was built in 1737 as a basin for the Old Dock and the Salthouse Dock followed in 1753. In fact neither dock was initially known by these names; Canning Dock was not named until its reconstruction in 1813 and Salthouse Dock was first called South Dock and renamed later in the century after the saltworks which stood nearby. There is also a street named after the salt works. The stretch of docks from Herculaneum, now filled, to the Pier Head has seen virtually no commercial traffic since the early 70s. Gone are the ships carrying

cargoes of fruit into the King's Docks which I myself remember unloading in 1969. As the docks fell into disrepair many fine buildings on the dock estate and the Dock Road went with them. For instance, the fine Dukes Dock warehouse, which was built by French prisoners of war in 1811, some 35 years earlier than the neighbouring Albert Dock warehouses, was demolished in 1966. But at last attitudes seem to be changing. The injection of central government funds via the Merseyside Development Corporation has provided money to buy the South Docks estate from the Mersey Docks and Harbour Company. The estate is now being reclaimed from dereliction and developed as a new industrial and recreation area. The flagship of this scheme is the Albert Dock where a massive restoration scheme is underway. It is a wonderful venture which not only preserves a major building but part of our maritime history at the same time. Both the Albert and the fine Wapping Warehouse have been threatened with demolition but their future is now secure.

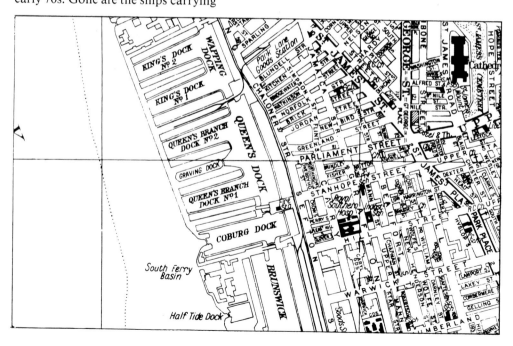

66

The tragedy is that so many buildings have already been lost. On the other side of the dock road virtually nothing is left of Liverpool's maritime history apart from street names and a handful of pubs and warehouses. All of what was once the heart of 'Sailor Town' around Canning Place has vanished. From the days of sail this district had a notorious reputation the world over but now no vestige of it remains. Many of these losses almost amount to vandalism on the part of the "City Fathers". It is only in the last decade that the authorities have woken up and are now striving to protect some of the remaining monuments to Liverpool's past. At least one corner of Liverpool, the Albert Dock, has some hope for the future.

**1** The dock road South of the city centre has several names: Strand Street, Wapping, Chaloner Street and finally Sefton Street. There was reputed to be a pub on almost every corner of which we show four. The first is the Queens Dock Hotel which ended its life as a canteen before demolition.

**2** The Brunswick known locally as the 'seven steps' is also named after an adjacent dock. This pub is still standing though empty and derelict.

**3** The Baltic Fleet pub is an imposing, listed building and the quality of its architecture has probably saved it. Renovations have been carried out since this photograph was taken in 1976.

**4** The Duke's Crown pub, though another fine building, failed to survive the new ring road scheme.

**5** In Park Lane stood what was latterly known as the Keans Hotel. This magnificent example of highly decorated Victorian building is sadly no longer standing. As the lettering shows it was originally built for a wine and spirits business who probably required premises close to the bonded warehouses at Albert Dock.

**6** This shot of the Baltic Ships Stores shows another building on Park Lane whose use was dock related.

**7** Behind this part of Park Lane is an area of municipal tenements. Kent Gardens from the 1930s is shown here and even this building has a maritime history. The flats occupy the former site of the Phoenix foundry where Merseyside's first marine engine was built. Lydia Anne Street was named after the foundry manager's wife.

**8** These tenements in the same area date from the 1920s and were amongst the first dwellings to replace the overcrowded, squalid courts that were rife in the district.

**9** Brick Street ran east-west between St James Street and Chaloner Street. Originally it was dense with the old Liverpool courts, later a mixture of industrial units and older municipal flats existed, such as Prince Albert Gardens on St. James Street shown during demolition in 1981.

**10** This once magnificent building on Hurst Street has also been lost. Pictured here at the end ot its life, this highly ornate piece of Victoriana would surely have been worth saving as its like will never be built again.

**11** The cross roads of Hurst Street and Salthouse Lane shows some of the original housing dating from the mid nineteenth century. These narrow houses had one room per floor built over cellars; they were not graced with rear windows.

**12** South Castle Street was almost totally destroyed by bombing during the last war. This last surviving block was destroyed by the planners and came down in 1975 and now the street itself no longer exists.

**13** King Street has also disappeared and these imposing warehouses made way for the 'Holiday Inn' Hotel.

**14** and **15** Opposite King Street stood Chapel Walk and Benn's Gardens; these narrow streets also tragically disappeared in the early 1970s with no thought of preserving these interesting buildings. The area had much charm and the fine terraces were used as small business premises. The two streets formed a four sided block opening off South Castle Street and were even enclosed with their own wrought iron gates.

**16** The Sailors Home dating from 1847, was one of Liverpool's most magnificent and well known buildings. The design of the interior was also interesting with decks reminiscent of sailing ships. It was demolished in 1973.

**17** The Flying Dutchman, named after a seafarers legend, stood close to the site of Liverpool's first dock at the corner of Canning Place and Litherland Alley.

**18** This warehouse stood on Crooked Lane until 1975. This winding alley was part of the network of lanes that existed in the Canning Place area. The Albert Dock is clearly visible in the background.

**19** and **20** These photographs show one of the few buildings that looks better in 1985 than it did in 1975. The Albert Dock warehouse complex is the largest single area of Grade I listed buildings in the country. Thanks to the intervention of the Merseyside Development Corporation the Albert Dock is being completely renovated and re-developed. It is once more buzzing with activity and will eventually house shops, offices, flats, restaurants and bars as well as the Tate Gallery Liverpool and the Maritime Museum.

Much of the old city centre has disappeared in the last twenty years as the photographs in this book remind us. Not only have we lost many fine buildings but thriving, bustling communities centred around markets have vanished too. The extent of the changes has often been drastic, as in Marybone; sometimes piecemeal, as in Tithebarn Street. For example the buildings opposite Exchange station have recently been cleared but fortunately the station's original facade has been restored and preserved as part of a new building complex which now stands on the site of the old station. Tithebarn Street is one of old Liverpool's original streets. Formerly known as Moor Street it was re-named after the erection of a tythe barn in 1523, probably on the site of Marybone's junction with Great Crosshall Street. Marybone was once a densely populated corner of the city, one of the poorest areas of nineteenth century Liverpool. Many of its streets have now disappeared under the new inner ring road.

Other areas have undergone changes perhaps less worthwhile. In Great Charlotte Street which formerly ran from Whitechapel to Ranelagh Street there used to be three

## City Centre

markets. Whilst several adjacent streets simply disappeared, Great Charlotte Street was reduced to a small section standing between Ranelagh Street and Elliot Street. These were some of the drastic clearances necessitated by the building of the huge St. John's Precinct. In the same period Queen Square with its fruit and vegetable market disappeared. For a short time I worked in this market and many people felt that its destruction was a sad end to a quaint old part of Liverpool. The bustling market with its colourful characters should have remained as part and parcel of everyday life of the city centre. Ironically it has since been declared that the square and its surrounding streets need not have been demolished at all. St. John's Lane still stands as a thorough-fare but only one of its buildings avoided the bulldozer and has since been renovated. Lime Street, probably Liverpool's most famous street, did not escape the re-development of the 1960's. The view of St. Georges Hall from the north end of Lime Street in 1964 (see photo) shows one of the huge Victorian blocks which was removed

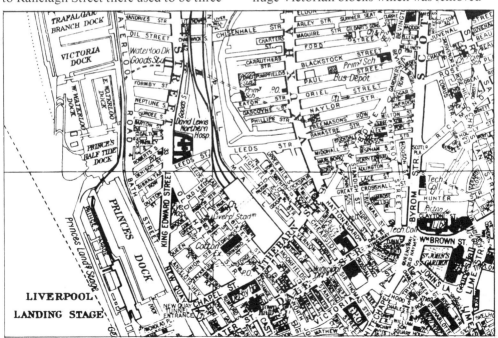

to make way for the St John's Precinct development. Lime Street took its name from the limekilns that stood here in the eighteenth century (the site of the present railway station). In recent years the street was one of Liverpool's most attractive by night, the neon lights helping to create its unique character. The character of the city centre in general is now much diminished compared with the 1960's and seems likely to decline further in the future.

Close to Lime Street stands Clayton Square where some of the structures are 200 years old. These buildings have been designated for demolition to make way for new shops. The thought of the remains of this Liverpool square being destroyed is diabolical. The lessons from the recent past are obviously still being ignored with the continued sweeping away of what little is left of Liverpool's character. Queen Square no longer exists; Williamson Square is but a shadow of its former self and it appears Clayton Square is destined for a similar fate.

**1** St. Paul's Square, photographed in 1966 is overshadowed by the John Moores Centre then under construction. Once the centre of Liverpool's Welsh community, the square took its name from St. Paul's Church erected here in 1769.

**2** The Greyhound pub, demolished in 1977, was at the corner of Tithebarn Street and Hatton Garden.

**3** The Justice Hotel photographed in splendid isolation in desolate Marybone, just prior to demolition in 1981.

**4** Stockdale Street, off Marybone. This terraced street was cleared in the late 1960's and the new inner ring road now runs across the ground upon which it once stood.

**5** Great Charlotte Street, one of a number of old market streets destroyed during the construction of the huge St. John's Precinct. In the foreground is the old pub 'The Spanish House Hotel', at the junction with Whitechapel. The Royal Court Theatre can be seen in the background. Photographed in 1970, this section of Great Charlotte Street is now a car park.

**6** The Stork Hotel, Queen Square. The hotel was a former town house, older than the property surrounding it, and is shown during demolition in 1976.

**7** Queen Square, off Great Charlotte Street, still had a fruit and vegetable market in the 1960's.

**8** St. John's Lane, named after a late 18th century church which once stood on the site of St. John's Gardens behind St. Georges Hall. The hotel, The Victoriana, at the junction with Roe Street, was demolished in 1965.

**9** Lime Street in 1964, showing St. Georges Hall. Beyond it stands one of the massive Victorian buildings which were later demolished to make way for St. John's Precinct.

St. George's Hall was completed in 1854 and at the present time stands empty, (let's hope our city fathers never allow this magnificent Victorian structure to decay and become another building that's finally as so many other examples in this book show, just came tumbling down).